This book belongs to

....

CONTENTS

Edited by Stephanie Milton. *Designed by* Martin Aggett.
Cover and Endpapers illustrated by Stuart Trotter.

A chance to win £150 of book tokens!
See page 69 for details.

NATIONAL BOOK tokens

THE RUPERT ANNUAL

EXPRESS NEWSPAPERS

EGMONT
We bring stories to life

Published in Great Britain 2013 by Egmont UK Limited
The Yellow Building, 1 Nicholas Road, London W11 4AN
Rupert Bear™ & © 2013 Classic Media Distribution Limited/Express Newspapers.
All Rights Reserved.

ISBN 978 1 4052 6765 6
54733/1
Printed in Italy

No. 78

RUPERT
Rugger

The adventure begins as Uncle Bruno's treat for Rupert and his chums. But a Rugger ball can cause a great deal of trouble, as Rupert finds out when he makes a forced journey to a far kingdom. Once there, he has to try very hard to explain a mistake.

RUPERT WELCOMES UNCLE BRUNO

The little pals are playing ball
When Rupert's Uncle gives a call.

He strides across the grassy patch,
"I'm off to watch a Rugger match!"

Spring is here and Rupert has been called for by his pals Bill Badger and Algy Pug. "Come on out," says Bill. "Algy's brought his ball. Last time we had a game of football you went off on an adventure with Rastus." "Ha, ha! Sorry about that," laughs Rupert. "Rastus isn't likely to turn up this morning. I've just seen him setting off with a rod and line for a day's fishing in Nutwood Lake. You're right about football, if we don't have a game soon it will be warm enough for cricket. I'll just get my scarf." They go to some open ground and scamper around happily until they are interrupted by a cheery shout and a large figure strides towards them. "Why, it's Uncle Bruno," Rupert smiles, as he runs forward. "D'you want me?" "Yes, your Mummy told me you were out playing with your chums," says Uncle, "so I came to find you."

and the Match

RUPERT RETURNS TO HIS CHUMS

"May I take Rupert in my car?"
Smiles Uncle Bruno. "It's not far."

Then Rupert runs to tell his news,
"Hi! You can join us, if you choose."

Uncle Bruno lifts Rupert up. "I'm taking a half day off to see my favourite Rugger club play its last game of the season," he says. "Would you like to come too?" "Ooo, yes please," says Rupert, eagerly. "I've no idea what a Rugger match is like. Do you think that Mummy and Daddy will let me go?" At the Bears' cottage permission is soon granted, and Uncle Bruno prepares to leave. "We mustn't delay," he says. "The match is due to start soon. If your pals would care to come you may ask them." "Thank you very much," cries Rupert. "That would be even more fun." He loses no time in dashing back to tell Algy and Bill his news. "Come on, you're invited to the Rugger match too!" he shouts. "Uncle says there is room for all of us in his car. Be quick, he's ready to go." "That's jolly kind of him," gasps Algy. "I'll leave my ball at your home while we're away."

RUPERT STARES AT THE GAME

They reach the Rugger pitch at last,
Gasps Rupert, "My, that game looks fast!"

The ball shoots straight towards the chums.
"Quick, duck!" cries Algy. "Here it comes!"

The muddy players dodge around,
And bring each other to the ground.

But when at length their rough game ends,
They all walk off, the best of friends.

Neither Bill nor Algy has ever seen a Rugger match, and they are keen to join Rupert, so Uncle Bruno piles them all into his car and drives them away. The Rugger match is in full swing when they arrive and walk towards the pitch. "There are not many people watching on this side of the field," says Uncle Bruno. "Let's stay here." All at once Rupert ducks as the ball passes over his head. "Is *that* the ball?" gasps Bill. "Why ever is it that shape? It's more like a sausage!" The young pals watch the game as it becomes still faster and more boisterous. "I say, there's not much football about this," says Rupert as he tries to follow the play. "They're handling all the time. And just look how they're knocking each other about! How they must hate each other!" But Bill only grins. "It must be a good lark," he chuckles. "I should love to tumble about like that!" At length the game comes to an end, and to Rupert's surprise they players walk off in the friendliest fashion.

RUPERT IS TAKEN TO A SHOP

"Now you shall have a ball the same,
So you can play a Rugger game."

An odd-shaped ball the shopman shows,
It is for Rugger, Rupert knows.

Near Nutwood, Uncle lets them out,
"Now practise kicking that about!"

When Algy kicks, the ball goes straight.
"Just try," he laughs. "It's simply great!"

On the way back to the car Rupert begs to be told the rules of the game they have just seen. Uncle Bruno gives a little laugh. "During the match I was too excited to explain things to you," he says. "Now perhaps you'd better start by seeing if you can kick a ball of that queer shape." He takes the little pals to the nearest sports shop. "Yes, sir," says the shopman. "Although the season is finishing I have just one junior Rugger ball left. Here it is – right weight – stronger than leather – never wants blowing up." Near the edge of the village Uncle Bruno leaves the three little pals. "Some day you may be big and strong enough to enjoy that game," he says, "but first you must learn how to kick that odd-shaped ball." Rupert thanks him for the fine present and then Uncle Bruno goes home. "Come on, let's try," says Algy, racing towards the Common. He gives the ball a big kick and away it flies just where he wants it to go. "Pooh, it's easy!" he laughs. "You just try."

RUPERT ENJOYS THE SCRAMBLE

Now nobody can kick it straight,
It twists and spins, at such a rate!

"Let's run with it!" They dodge and pass,
And tumble, sprawling, on the grass.

Laughs Bill, "I've mud all over me!"
Then someone calls, "Come here, you three!"

"What's happened? I don't understand!"
Cries Mummy, shopping-bag in hand.

Seeing how easily Algy has kicked the new ball Rupert has a kick at it, then Bill tries, then Algy tries again, but now nobody can do it properly. The ball spins and twists and glances away and goes in every direction except the one they wish. "Your first kick must have been a lucky accident, Algy," says Rupert. "Yes, let's play the other sort of Rugger," suggests Bill. So they try to run with the ball and dodge and bring each other down. "This is better than I expected," grins Algy as he goes sprawling.

The ground under the grass is soft and the little pals tumble about until they are breathless. They are just about to laugh at each other because of the mess they are in when a sudden call startles them and Mrs. Bear appears. She stares in horror. *"What on earth have you been doing?"* she demands. "Where have you been? I've been expecting you for ever so long! Why didn't Uncle Bruno bring you home? Come along this minute." She grabs Rupert, and Bill and Algy creep away.

RUPERT IS ALLOWED TO GO OUT

"Just wait till I see Uncle next!"
Frowns Mrs. Bear, she sounds quite vexed.

So Rupert's made to work instead,
Then finishes the day in bed!

Next morning, Mummy says he may,
If he keeps clean, go out to play.

Once more, the new ball twists and twirls,
Back over Rupert's head it curls!

Mrs. Bear grips Rupert firmly and marches him smartly home. He tries to tell her about the game of Rugger and about the sports shop, and he shows her the new ball, but she is too angry to listen closely. "I've never seen you in such a mess," she says grimly. "Just wait until I see Uncle Bruno again! I'll give him a piece of my mind for leading you into such a game! You come home now and help me with my work. Then straight to bed while I wash your clothes!" Poor Rupert obeys without a word. Next morning he is very, very good until he sees Mrs. Bear comfortably settled in a chair. "Please may I go out and practise kicking my new ball?" he pleads, "I'll promise not to tumble about or get muddy." Mrs. Bear pauses. "You may go for an hour if you promise not to play with those two rips, Bill and Algy," she says. They're still in disgrace with me." Rupert agrees and soon he is out and finding the ball as difficult as ever to kick.

RUPERT UPSETS THE BIRDS

It bounces, zigzag, down a slope,
"That bush has caught it up, I hope!"

As Rupert tries to get it back,
Two screeching birds swoop on his track.

He grabs his ball, then turns and finds
Excited birds of many kinds.

They screech and squawk, then off they skim,
While one small bird keeps watch on him.

Rupert has chosen a lonely spot high on the Common to avoid the chance of meeting Bill and Algy, and, as before, he cannot make the ball go up, but it curls back over his head and bounces crookedly down a bank. It is only after a long search that he spies it lodged in a bush. As he bends forward to reach it, a loud screeching by his ear makes him stop. With a startled jump he looks and sees two birds close by. "Whatever is the matter with them?" he mutters.

After a while the two small birds fly off and Rupert pushes his way into the bush. Though the ball is awkwardly placed, he reaches it, and is just emerging when the birds return with dozens of others of all sizes who squawk round him in great excitement. "What on earth *is* the matter?" he says. "I'm not trespassing, am I?" They do not attack him, so he climbs back again. At that the birds change their plan. The main flock flies off, leaving one bird to watch Rupert.

RUPERT HAS A SUDDEN SCARE

"I wonder what can be amiss,"
Gasps Rupert Bear. "I don't like this!"

Right in his path a huge bird lands,
"How did that fall into your hands?"

"Your Uncle! Don't tell fairy tales!"
And gripping Rupert, off it sails!

The great bird soars to such a height
That Rupert drops his ball in fright.

Rupert is relieved that most of the birds have gone, but their behaviour has been so peculiar that he is uneasy and he decides to hurry away from that part of the Common. As he trots steadily on he does not realise that the flock has returned until a huge form appears, and the largest bird he has ever seen perches on a boulder in his path. "Stop, how did you get that?" demands the bird. "Oh my, can you *speak*?" quavers Rupert. "My Uncle Bruno gave it to me. It-it's for playing Rugger."

The great bird glares at Rupert. "You're telling stories!" it declares. "No uncle gave it to you. You found it in a bush. You were seen! Come, this won't do at all. It's too important. You must answer to another." Next moment Rupert finds himself seized and swung into the air. "Hi, put me down," he squeals. "I've no idea what you're talking about!" But the bird only flies higher and higher. Rupert drops the ball and does not see that another big bird swoops after it.

RUPERT DROPS INTO A NEST

Beyond wild peaks, his captor swerves,
Around a grove of pines it curves.

It finds a strange nest, deep and wide,
And drops the little bear inside.

A tiny bird keeps watch again,
But it refuses to explain.

The anxious little bear creeps out,
He hopes that someone is about.

Rupert's alarming journey takes him away from all the country that he knows. The grip of the great bird is firm without hurting the little bear, who gradually becomes less frightened as he is carried past a great range of mountains and towards a forest of pine trees. Over one of the highest trees the bird swerves from its direct flight and circles slowly. "There's a huge nest just below us," thinks Rupert. No sooner has he spotted it than the strong claws relax their hold and he drops straight into it. Although the nest is so big it is lined with lots of mosses and soft grasses, so that Rupert is not bruised at all, and when he has recovered his wits, he pulls himself the right way up and gazes round him. He is still being watched by a small bird. "Why am I being treated like this?" he demands. "Whose nest is this?" The bird answers nothing and screwing up his courage Rupert steps carefully on to a branch to see if he can recognise the way he has come.

RUPERT FEELS SO UNHAPPY

"That bird!" gasps Rupert in surprise,
"It's found my Rugger ball!" he cries.

At once, two screeching birds protest,
They drive him back into the nest.

As Rupert sinks back, in despair,
A voice calls, "Greetings, little bear!"

The newcomer has long, thin legs,
"Pardon our rudeness, please!" it begs.

The branch sways in the slight wind and Rupert has to hold on tight. "There's no way down," he moans. 'And I couldn't find a road home even if I reached the ground. Those awful mountains!" All at once he stares as another flock of birds appears, flying fast, and the largest has something in its beak. "That's my new ball, the Rugger one!" he exclaims. "How ever did he find it?" Hardly had he spoken when two smaller birds come at him screeching and driving him back into the huge nest. They squawk angrily at Rupert for some time before flying after the flock, leaving a smaller one still watching him. "Oh, this is hopeless," sighs Rupert miserably. "What *is* the matter with them all? Why have they carried me off?" Then a shadow falls across him and the branch sways again as a large, long-legged bird perches right beside him. "Little bear, I bring you greetings," says the newcomer. "We fear you have been treated very rudely and we are sorry."

RUPERT BEGS TO GO HOME

"You are of great importance now,"
The bird tells Rupert, with a bow.

A flock of birds comes into range.
Beneath them flutters something strange.

A dozen birds hold one cord each,
And bring a strong sheet into reach.

"You shall go home, but not just yet,"
The large bird squawks. "Now, in you get!"

Rupert is astonished at the kind tone of his latest visitor after the angry squawking of the others. "Yes, it was awful," he says. "I was terribly scared and I can't understand why I was carried away. May I go home now?" "Be patient, little bear," says the other, bowing very politely. "You shall go home, but not yet. You have become too important to us." "B-but I'm only Rupert Bear of Nutwood; I'm not important to anybody," says Rupert. "Oh yes you are," says the bird. "Just look at the sky over there." High in the sky another smaller flock of birds has appeared with something underneath them. As they draw near Rupert sees that it is a sort of sheet held by a dozen cords, and a bird is holding the top of each cord. Nearer they come until they are overhead with the sheet resting near to Rupert. "Come on. In you get," says the big bird. "That will be more comfy for you than the first part of your journey!" Warily Rupert clambers along the branch to inspect the sheet.

RUPERT REACHES A CASTLE

Then Rupert, safe, though ill at ease,
Is swept away across the trees.

They reach a castle, hid in cloud,
Where stands a guard, so stiff and proud.

Gently, those birds let down the sheet,
Then Rupert scrambles to his feet.

The King's chief Herald, with a smile,
Bids Rupert rest himself a while.

Rupert gazes nervously into the sheet. "I can't get home and I can't stay here in the tree," he thinks. "If this is what they want me to do I'd better do it," and he slides in between the cords. As soon as they feel his weight the birds carrying the sheet fly off, led by the big one. "Oh dear, this is more comfortable than being carried by a bird's claws," thinks Rupert, "but it doesn't feel any safer!" Up they go until a vast castle appears partly hidden in clouds. A guard stands on a wall waiting for them. The birds let the sheet down and gently, with the tiniest bump, Rupert finds himself sitting on a high terrace. The cords fall around him and the dozen birds who have held them flutter down to make sure he is not hurt. As he picks himself up a strange official-looking bird struts forward. "You are welcome, little bear," says the odd creature. "Very welcome indeed. I trust you enjoyed your journey." "Well, no, I didn't," says Rupert. "Why am I here?"

RUPERT IS TREATED KINDLY

"Come, little bear, your strength renew,
Before your royal interview!"

For his refreshment, Rupert finds
Delicious fruit of many kinds.

"The King requests your presence, so,
If you are ready, we will go."

The King, in gorgeous raiment clad,
With all his courtiers, looks so glad.

The bird inclines its head towards Rupert. "I am His Majesty's chief Herald," it says. "I therefore bid you welcome and invite you to prepare for a royal interview, but first you must need refreshments after your difficult journey. Be so kind as to follow me." It makes its dignified way along a corridor, and Rupert follows. Other strange little creatures accompany them, until they all reach a table holding beautiful fruit. There two kindly penguins wait on Rupert to see that he has all the refreshments he wants. Though Rupert asks all sorts of questions to find out why he has been brought so far, the waiting penguins refuse to answer any of them and he remains as mystified as ever. At length the figure of one of the guards appears in the doorway. "If the little bear is refreshed will he kindly come with me," says the great bird respectfully, and again Rupert is led to a tower where he sees other creatures around the gorgeous figure of the King of the Birds.

RUPERT FOLLOWS THE KING

*"Bird-nesting! That's a dreadful case!
But we shan't keep you in disgrace."*

*"We took into account, you see,
Your wonderful discovery!"*

*How pleased that learned parrot seems,
"Now, tell us all you know," it beams.*

*The King says, "Take a careful look,
Then give us details for our book."*

At Rupert's approach all the courtiers give way so that he can go right up to the royal presence. "Ah, 'tis our little bear," says the King affably. "Now you can tell us all. We have decided to forgive you the serious crime of bird-nesting because of your wonderful discovery! Come, we will go to my Records Office." A solemn procession forms up, and Rupert marches with the King, but he is as puzzled as ever. "What on earth is he talking about?" he thinks. "I can't understand it. I've never been bird-nesting in my life!" The King of the Birds leads the way into a large office, and Rupert finds himself facing a learned-looking parrot, who gazes at him keenly. "Ah, the little bear, himself! Good, good," says the parrot. "Your discovery is most important. Be sure you tell us all you know and my clerk shall enter every detail in this book." Still bewildered Rupert is led out and they watch another stately bird approaching with something on a velvet cushion.

RUPERT SAYS IT'S A JOKE

"How splendid!" Rupert laughs. "That's mine!"
"Yes," says the King. "That egg is fine!"

"The bird that laid it must be rare,
What did it look like, little bear?"

"But that is not an egg at all!"
Smiles Rupert. "It's my Rugger ball!"

"How dare you contradict our King!
His Majesty knows everything!"

While all sorts of birds cluster around in excitement, the cushion is put down before the King and Rupert gazes at the object on it. Then he gives a happy cry. "Why, it's *mine*!" he laughs. "Yes," says the King. "It is yours. When you were bird-nesting you were observed to pick it out of a bush. We have never seen an egg like that. You are the only person to tell us what bird laid it. All the birds are my subjects, and this must be a very, very rare one that we don't know." While the King stares at him, Rupert capers about in delight at what has happened. "This is a lovely joke!" he cries. "My pal Bill Badger said it looked like a sausage, and now you call it an egg! It isn't an egg. It's my Rugger ball, and ..." He gets no further, for on the instant he is surrounded by screaming, hissing, frowning birds who push him away. "How dare you contradict our King?" screeches the biggest one. "No bird ever dreams of doing so. I never heard such impudence!"

RUPERT STAYS IN A CELL

The birds drive Rupert Bear away,
"Of course it is an egg!" they say.

Into a small, bare cell he's cast,
The door is slammed, and bolted fast.

"They simply wouldn't let me speak!"
Then Rupert hears an anxious squeak.

"Who are you?" asks the nervous mouse.
"I don't want you to share my house."

All the birds surrounding the King are suddenly shocked and angry, and a stern guard drives Rupert right away. "B-but, what have I *done*?" quavers the little bear. "I only told the truth." "Stuff and nonsense," says the guard. "A king's a king. And if the King says it is an egg, it *is* an egg! Who are you to contradict? Now you go in there until you cool down and until we decide your punishment." Rupert is pushed very firmly by a big wing into a small, bare cell, and the door is slammed. Finding himself shut in Rupert sits down on a bench and holds his head in his hands. "This is all mad," he moans. "Where am I now? Is this a prison?" A slight noise makes him glance down, and he sees a large mouse peeping at him round a water jug. "Who are you? Why are you here?" squeaks the mouse, leaping nervously to the floor. "Go away. This is my home, and I don't like any company." "I wish I *could* go away!" says Rupert. "But how can I?"

RUPERT EXPLAINS THE MISTAKE

Some tiny, chirping birds appear,
They ask, "What are you doing here?"

So Rupert sits down, sad at heart,
And tells his story from the start.

"We'll gladly help you, if we can,"
Then each tries hard to form a plan.

"Our giant hen, we'll tell the King,
Should try and hatch that ball-egg thing!"

Before the mouse can reply more noise comes from the other direction as some tiny, chattering birds fly in between the bars of the cell. "Hey, what's going on?" chirrups the first one. "We weren't there when it all happened. Do tell us, who are you? And why have they put you in here? Have you been terribly bad?" "I don't think I've been bad at all!" says Rupert. And he tells them all the things that have happened since he went to practise Rugger kicks on Nutwood Common that morning. The tiny bird looks very concerned at Rupert's story. "You've had bad luck," says one of them, "but you *should* have known better than to contradict a king! Now the question is, how are we going to get you out?" They fall silent while Rupert and the mouse walk up and down deep in thought. All at once two of the birds take to the air. "We've had an idea," they squeak. "If that thing is an egg it could be hatched by our giant hen. We'll ask the King."

RUPERT WAITS A LONG TIME

"If it's a ball, she's sure to fail,
The King will then believe your tale."

"He will admit that he was wrong,
And you shall be set free, ere long."

A guard stalks in, he looks so stern,
"His Majesty bids you return."

The stately bird goes on ahead,
And up a stairway Rupert's led.

Rupert is slow to grasp the birds' idea, but the mouse squeaks up at once. "It's jolly good," he says. "If the King is proved wrong about that ball-egg thing you will be set free, and I shall have my home here to myself again. Get on with it, and I hope the hatching won't take a week!" "It wouldn't hatch in five years," says Rupert glumly, turning to the window as the birds fly out. "If you do speak to the King, please tell him I'm very sorry I upset him." When the tiny birds have gone, there is silence for a long time while Rupert waits anxiously. Then suddenly there is a click and a creak, the cell door is swung open, and in stalks one of the guards still looking very unfriendly. "Little bear, you are bidden again to the presence of His Majesty," he says. "What does he want me for now?" asks Rupert. "Silence! No questions," says the guard sternly. "Follow me and delay not!" And he goes ahead to another tower and up a flight of steps.

23

RUPERT MEETS THE GIANT HEN

*"Ah," says the King, "I'm told we ought
To hatch this splendid egg you brought."*

*"And so," he smiles, "I mean to ask
Our giant hen to do this task."*

*"This egg is rare and precious, yes!
Please hatch it with great gentleness."*

*"This is no egg!" the huge hen snaps.
"You thought you'd trick us all, perhaps!"*

Again Rupert finds himself facing the royal group. He doesn't quite know what to say, and is very relieved when the King of the Birds seems not to expect him to talk at all. The gorgeous bird isn't nearly as angry as the birds who hustled Rupert away, and he retires to his throne. The cushion carrying the Rugger ball is in front of him. "So we meet again, little bear," he says genially. "Now about this egg, look who's coming." And at Rupert's side appears the largest hen he has ever seen. The King rises from his throne and addresses the hen. "Here we have an egg such as we have never seen before," he says. "It was brought by the little bear here, and must be very, very rare and precious. I wish you'd hatch it with the greatest of care." The giant hen walks round it slowly, touching it gently and squinting at it. Then she straightens up. "Is the little bear trying to be funny?" she says. "This is no egg! However long I sit on it, it won't hatch."

RUPERT PREPARES FOR A KICK

"It's not an egg, I know full well,
The thing is just a hollow shell."

"Alas, my hopes were all in vain,
I have no precious egg, it's plain!"

The little bear cries, "Never mind,
That ball is quite a special kind!"

To help the King forget his woes,
Some Rugger practice Rupert shows.

The King and his courtiers cluster round the giant hen after the extraordinary thing she has said. "Oh dear," thinks Rupert, "is she going to be put in prison too? The King said it was an egg and she said it wasn't!" But she seems to be a very favoured person and soon the worried King is turning to Rupert. "Our giant hen knows more about eggs than anybody in my kingdom," he says. "She must be right. But if it isn't an egg what on earth *is* it?" Rupert is excited at the way things have turned out. "I was trying to tell Your Majesty when I was hustled away," he says. "It's a sort of ball for playing a game called Rugger. I was practising kicking when I came here. Do let me show you." "Oh, very well," says the King. "Though it sounds rather mad!" He hurriedly collects the surrounding birds and marches them all, except the giant hen, away to a safe distance while Rupert removes the ball from the cushion and prepares to take a running kick at it.

RUPERT RUNS TO THE EDGE

He kicks the ball and shouts, "That's fine!
Just look, it's going straight in line."

"Of all the mad games to invent!"
The hen squawks, in astonishment.

"The wind has caught my Rugger ball!"
Gasps Rupert Bear. "And there's no wall!"

The ball rolls off, as he arrives,
But in pursuit, a large bird dives.

Rupert kicks the Rugger ball as hard as he can and the watching birds jump nervously as if they expect to see it break into pieces. "Hooray, that's the first time I've made it go where I wanted," chuckles the little bear. "Well, and what next?" demands the giant hen who has stayed near him. "D'you mean to say that they take all that trouble to make that thing just so that it can be kicked?"

"Yes, and it's grand fun," says Rupert. "Pah, you earth people are all mad!" squawks the hen.

Rupert starts to tell the giant hen all about the excitement of a Rugger match and of the difficulty of kicking straight, and she looks more puzzled than before. All at once Rupert stops. "My Rugger ball!" he gasps. "The wind's carrying it farther than I meant it to go. There's no wall around this terrace. It will go over!" Dashing forward he just misses it. As he throws himself full length the ball drops into the clouds. One of the largest birds has spotted it and plunges in pursuit.

RUPERT BOUNCES THE BALL

"You kicked it, yet it didn't crack!"
Exclaims the monarch, coming back.

"It's made of plastic, that is why."
And Rupert makes the ball bounce high.

"Remarkable! What is it for?"
So Rupert tells his tale once more.

The monarch listens in delight.
He laughs, "We'll have to put things right!"

Rupert pulls himself cautiously back from the edge and walks across the terrace. The King and his courtiers gradually get over their nervousness and return from their high platform just as the plunging bird arrives with the Rugger ball in its beak. The King still can't get it out of his head that it is some sort of egg. "Why didn't it crack when you kicked it?" he asks. "It's not meant to," says Rupert. And he shows them how high it will bounce. When the King slowly realises that the Rugger ball is not an egg and that it won't explode or even crack, he shows great interest. "I'm disappointed that this doesn't belong to one of my very rare subjects," he says, "but you must tell me just what it is for." So, at last, Rupert is able to explain what has happened since Uncle Bruno took him and his two chums to the Rugger match. The King listens attentively, and the courtiers all seem very amused as Rupert is escorted away in the middle of the royal party.

RUPERT LEAVES FOR NUTWOOD

"To show we blamed you wrongfully,
Our guest of honour you shall be."

"Goodbye! We're very glad you came,
For now we know about your game."

"Stand on this sheet, please!" Rupert's told,
Then once again twelve birds take hold.

"At home, I'll have a tale to tell!"
Smiles Rupert, as he waves farewell.

Instead of being taken to a prison cell Rupert finds himself now the guest of honour, and is offered more wonderful fruit. "Oh dear, I've already had one good meal!" he laughs. "You must be made strong for your return home," says the King. "Your story has been very funny. So you were *not* bird-nesting when you were seen in that bush. What a lot of misunderstanding started from that one mistake!" At length he waves goodbye. "Thank you for telling us about Rugger," he adds, as Rupert is led away. Rupert wonders how he is going to be sent home, and he feels nervous when he sees that the sheet that carried him before is still lying on the terrace. As he steps on to it the little lifting birds grab the cords. "You look awfully small to lift a heavy bear like me," he murmurs. "Are you sure you can do it again?" "There are twelve of us," says one of them. "Between us we could carry double your weight." In a moment Rupert is on his way.

RUPERT'S PALS GATHER ROUND

"Have you seen Rupert, anyone?"
Calls Pong-Ping, then he shouts, "Quick, run!"

"Rupert! You gave us such a shock!"
Gasps Bill, crouched down behind a rock.

"You landed safely! We're so glad!
But that's the second fright we've had."

"The largest bird we've ever seen
Swooped straight at us, across the green."

Bill Badger and Algy Pug have been searching for Rupert and wishing he'd bring that Rugger ball out again. They ask Rex Rabbit and Pong-Ping, but neither has seen the little bear. "Algy and I have had a fright this morning," says Bill. "We were ..." Before he can finish he has another shock, for a curious shape appearing in the sky makes them all bolt for cover. Next minute Rupert lands safely, the sheet is whisked away, and the first thing he sees is the scared face of Bill peeping over a boulder. In his joy to be back near his home Rupert sits on the boulder to recover his breath, and gradually his pals come out from their hiding place to crowd round him. "What on earth have you been playing at?" demands Bill. "How did you persuade the birds to carry you around like that? And, talking of birds, that is the second fright we've had inside an hour. When we were up on the higher part of the Common an enormous bird plunged straight at us and scared us away!"

RUPERT IS GLAD TO BE BACK

Round Rupert's head some small birds glide,
It's clear they mean to be his guide.

Now Rupert gives a joyful call,
"That huge bird brought my Rugger ball!"

Laughs Rex, "We'll all go home with you,
To hear the whole adventure through!"

The pals run homeward in a row,
And kick the new ball as they go.

At the mention of the large bird Rupert becomes alert. "What shape was it?" he asks. "Was it carrying anything?" As he speaks some small birds arrive and swirl around his head, squawking. "Hello, those look like the ones that first found me in the bush," he mutters. "Look, they're flying off towards the place where the huge bird was," says Algy. With a sudden idea Rupert dashes off after them and finds the little birds fluttering round and round his lost Rugger ball which is lying in the grass. Rupert hugs his new-found ball in delight. "Come on now, tell us what it all means," says Rex. "Oo, it's too long a story!" laughs Rupert. "Let's go home first and then you shall hear it all. Mummy said I wasn't to play with Bill and Algy today, but she won't mind when she hears it all. Then I must let Uncle Bruno know everything that has happened since he took us to that Rugger match!" And running in a row the little pals race homewards kicking the new ball as they go.

RUPERT and the Baby Cloud

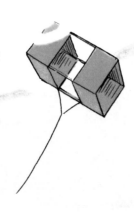

The strong wind tugs at Rupert's kite,
"Look out!" calls Algy. "Hold on tight!"

When Rupert Bear is carried up,
He's quickly rescued by the pup.

It is a windy day with grey clouds scudding across the sky, and Rupert sets off to sail his kite. "I'll look for a spot where there aren't any large trees," he thinks. Soon he finds just the right place on top of a hill.

He unwinds the string and as he launches his kite the wind lifts it into the air. The little bear is so busy that he does not notice Algy running towards him.

At that moment a strong gust of wind lifts the kite still higher, carrying Rupert off the ground! "Hang on, I'm coming," yells Algy. Racing up, he grabs Rupert and pulls with all his might.

31

RUPERT LOOKS INSIDE HIS KITE

With Algy's help it's not so hard,
They haul the kite in yard by yard.

Then Rupert stares and gives a cry—
"A cloud has come down from the sky!"

The little cloud holds so much rain,
It cannot float back home again.

From high above a cloud looks down,
And Algy's sure he sees it frown!

The little pup manages to get Rupert back to the ground. "Whew! Thanks, Algy," gasps Rupert. "You were just in time." They haul in the string and soon the kite is lying beside them. "Look, Algy, there's something inside it," cries Rupert. The two chums peer closely and there, trapped inside the kite, is a tiny grey cloud. "Goodness, how did it get in there?" gasps Algy. "The wind must have blown it inside," says Rupert, and he shakes the kite to free the little cloud.

Rupert lifts the cloud expecting it to float away, but it sinks to the ground. "I think I know the reason," he sighs. "It is heavy with rain. You can tell by the colour, it's such a dark grey. I'd better take it home with me. We can't leave it here." Algy carries the kite while his chum carefully holds the cloud. "Poor thing," says Rupert, "it's just a baby." Then Algy calls out: "Rupert, I believe one of the big clouds is frowning at us for taking the little cloud away. We'd better hurry."

RUPERT GOES OUT AT NIGHT

"Why, goodness me!" gasps Mrs Bear,
"Now what on earth have you got there?"

It's time for bed and last of all,
The cloud is left beside the wall.

Late in the night, a ladder drops,
And down the rungs a stranger hops.

The little person says, "Oh dear,
My precious soap is lost, I fear."

When Rupert enters his cottage Mrs Bear nearly drops her spectacles in surprise. "Well! You have brought home some strange things, but this is the first time you've come back with a cloud," she exclaims. Rupert explains how he came to find it and his Mummy says he must take good care of it. "I'll keep it near me so that no harm comes to it," he says. So when he goes to bed that night he puts the baby cloud in the corner of the bedroom. "That's a nice safe place," he murmurs sleepily.

During the night, Rupert awakens to see a ladder hanging near his window. Getting up, he creeps out to the garden and there, climbing down the ladder, is a strange little person dressed in oilskins and a sou'wester. "H-hallo, who are you?" asks Rupert. "Oh, I'm the Cloud-scrubber," is the reply. "My job is to keep the clouds clean. But I've lost my special soap. I dropped it somewhere near here. Will you help me look for it?" The two search carefully, but there is no sign of the soap.

RUPERT FOLLOWS THE BUBBLES

"If you should find it, let me know,"
He adds, as he's about to go.

Next morning, Rupert's full of hope
And says, "I'll try to find the soap."

A trail of bubbles gives the clue,
"Why, Edward!" Rupert cries. "It's you!"

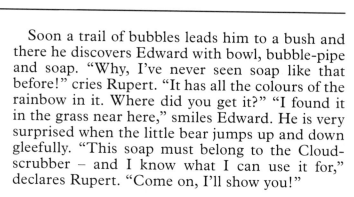

"This soap must be the special kind,"
Says Rupert. "What a lucky find!"

Oh well, I suppose I'll have to go back without it," says the Cloud-scrubber glumly. "If I wait any longer that cloud will carry my ladder out of reach." Waving goodbye to Rupert, he starts to climb the ladder. Only when he has disappeared does Rupert realise that he has not asked about the baby cloud. "I wish I'd remembered to tell the Cloud-scrubber," he thinks as he goes back to his room. Next morning he tells his mother what happened during the night. "So I'm going to see if I can find the soap," he says.

Soon a trail of bubbles leads him to a bush and there he discovers Edward with bowl, bubble-pipe and soap. "Why, I've never seen soap like that before!" cries Rupert. "It has all the colours of the rainbow in it. Where did you get it?" "I found it in the grass near here," smiles Edward. He is very surprised when the little bear jumps up and down gleefully. "This soap must belong to the Cloud-scrubber – and I know what I can use it for," declares Rupert. "Come on, I'll show you!"

RUPERT SETS THE CLOUD FREE

His story of the baby cloud,
Makes Edward blink and gasp aloud.

"That's right," says Mummy with a smile,
"Just leave the cloud to soak awhile."

"It's white as snow," says Rupert Bear,
"And see – it's floating in the air!"

They go outside. "I'll set it free,
Now watch," laughs Rupert gleefully.

I don't think you should have run off with it like that," grumbles Edward, "just when I was blowing my biggest bubbles." But Rupert soon puts matters right by explaining about the Cloud-scrubber and the baby cloud. When they arrive at the cottage they go into the kitchen. "Will you do some washing for me, Mummy?" asks Rupert. "Of course, dear," answers Mrs Bear. "There is plenty of hot water." Rupert fetches the baby cloud from his bedroom, and Edward watches him dip it in the sink.

"The Cloud-scrubber said that he used this special soap to clean the clouds, so it should be all right for this baby cloud," murmurs Rupert. When Mrs Bear returns she begins to wash the cloud. Before long its greyness disappears and it becomes white and fluffy. "My! How light it is," says Mrs Bear. "Now we can take it into the garden and let it float away," says Rupert happily. He carries the little cloud outside and throws it into the air. It rises slowly, tinged pink by the rays of the sun.

RUPERT RECEIVES A MESSAGE

Up goes the cloud, yet higher still,
The sight gives both the chums a thrill.

Then to the kite the soap is tied.
Says Rupert, "It's quite safe inside."

They hope the idea hasn't failed,
When high aloft the kite has sailed.

The words of thanks are all they need,
To make them pleased with their good deed!

The chums watch for a long time as the cloud floats higher and higher until it joins company with a passing cloud. "Now what's Rupert up to?" thinks Edward as his chum suddenly hurries indoors. In a few moments Rupert is back with his kite and a small parcel. "I've wrapped the soap in this parcel and if we tie it inside the kite we can send it back to my friend the Cloud-scrubber," he explains to Edward. "That big cloud overhead is where he is likely to be."

Presently the kite is hidden in the cloud above them. "I hope he is there," murmurs Rupert. After a while they pull the kite down and the parcel is no longer in it. "So the Cloud-scrubber must have taken the soap," says Edward. "And just look, he has written a message." On the side of the kite in big letters are the words THANK YOU. At that moment Algy comes running up the garden path. "We've got lots to talk about. Come inside and we'll tell you everything," laughs Rupert.

RUPERT

and the
Go-Kart Race

Story devised and illustrated by Stuart Trotter.

Says Mr Bear, "Oh, come and see,
What they are showing on TV!"

A motor race is on today.
It isn't very far away!

"Oh, may I go?" is Rupert's plea.
"As long as you are home for tea!"

And Rupert's pals are keen to come,
So off they trot to join the fun!

It is a crisp autumn afternoon and Rupert and his daddy are having a quiet afternoon in. Mr Bear is reading the paper whilst watching television. Rupert is engrossed in his latest project – making an origami paper banger which will make a noise like a thunder clap when pulled through the air. "Don't you want to watch this motor car race on television?" Mr Bear asks Rupert. Rupert looks up, and is very excited when he sees the race is nearby.

"Oh, please may I go and watch?" Rupert asks. "Of course," Mr Bear smiles. "Just make sure you're home in time for tea!" Rupert promises he will, and dashes out of the house as fast as he can. As he is racing across the common he spots his pals Bill, Podgy and Edward Trunk, and stops to say hello. "Where are you dashing off to?" Edward Trunk asks. Of course, when Rupert tells them about the race they all want to come along. So the pals set off together.

RUPERT MEETS JEROME

They climb into a nearby tree,
From where they watch the race with glee.

They have a truly perfect view
Of all the cars and drivers, too!

To their delight, the winner comes
To meet them, when the race is run.

The friendly driver, named Jerome,
Says he will drive them all back home.

The pals reach the other side of the common, and find a tree from which they have a perfect view of the race. They settle themselves on the lower branches and peer through the leaves.

"Oh, it looks like such fun!" Rupert gasps, watching the motor cars race past. "Doesn't it just!" Podgy agrees. "What a brilliant job!" The race is very exciting, and when it is finished, the pals dash onto the course to take a closer look at the cars.

They are very excited to see the winning driver heading over to speak to them! "Hello!" he greets them cheerily. "Did you watch the race?"

"Oh, yes, Sir!" Rupert replies. "It was wonderful!" The driver chuckles, and introduces himself as Jerome. "I bet you've never sat in a real racing car before," he says. "Would you like a ride home in mine?"

"Yes please!" the pals squeak.

RUPERT RIDES IN A RACING CAR

The pals climb in. Oh, what a treat!
Reclining in the comfy seat.

And soon they're back at Rupert's place.
"Why don't we have our own kart race?"

The pals head home to make their karts,
But where will Rupert get the parts?

Says Mrs Bear, "Although it's late,
Nice Mr Chimp might have a crate."

The pals jump in, and squeal in excitement as the driver revs the engine and sets off. But the journey home ends far too soon. The driver drops them at Rupert's house and leaves with a cheery wave. "I've an idea!" Rupert announces. "Let's have a go-kart race on Saturday!" The others agree. Edward and Bill already have go-karts, but Podgy and Rupert will have to build theirs from scratch. Rupert says a hasty goodbye – he wants to start designing his immediately.

Rupert dashes into the house, finds his sketchpad and pencils and sets to work at the kitchen table. Mrs Bear sees him drawing, and comes to take a look. "Why, it's perfect!" Mrs Bear says. "But we haven't any parts – why don't you go and see Mr Chimp at his shop? He'll most likely have a spare crate you can use."

"Thank you, Mummy, what a good idea!" Rupert smiles. He sets down his pencils and runs out of the door.

RUPERT FINDS A CRATE

But Podgy's beaten Rupert there,
And Rupert's starting to despair.

Then Rupert sees one final crate,
But it's reserved and he's too late!

"What shall I do?" poor Rupert moans.
"I'll never find a crate!" he groans.

But then a truck comes round the bend,
And something drops from its back end.

Rupert dashes down the lane to Mr Chimp's shop as fast as he can. He arrives just in time to see Podgy leaving, and he has a crate! This looks promising! Rupert says hello to his pal, then follows Mr Chimp inside. There's one crate left, and he asks Mr Chimp if he may have it.

"I'm terribly sorry, Rupert, that crate is for PC Growler," Mr Chimp replies. "He's due to pick it up any moment." Rupert is crestfallen – if only there had been one more spare crate!

Rupert thanks Mr Chimp politely, and wanders sadly out of the shop and back down the lane. He has no idea where he'll find a crate now – how will he ever make a go-kart in time for the race? A truck passes him as he is trudging along the road, lost in thought. There is a bend in the road up ahead and as the truck rounds the corner something falls off the back. It looks like a box of some kind. Not daring to believe his luck, Rupert goes to investigate what it is.

RUPERT DISTURBS THE IMPS

Young Rupert can't believe his luck.
A crate has fallen off the truck!

And Rupert all at once can see,
This box will suit him perfectly!

He drags the crate away with him
Across the common. What a din!

An Imp of Spring appears nearby.
"What are you doing?" is his cry.

Rupert crouches down and peers into the bushes where the item landed. To his delight, he discovers it is an empty crate! Rupert is amazed at his luck – the crate will do nicely for his go-kart! Smiling happily, Rupert drags the crate out of the tall grass by the road and sets off for home. He can already picture his brilliant go-kart! All he needs now are some wheels.

Lost in thought, he makes his way across Nutwood Common, dragging the crate over the grass. Suddenly, an angry little figure appears in a nearby tree – it is one of the Imps of Spring! "What are you doing?" the Imp hisses. "You're destroying the grass and flowers with that crate! And you're making an enormous racket. What are you playing at?" Then two more Imps appear, looking very angry also.

RUPERT IS TAKEN UNDERGROUND

"I'm sorry! What more can I say?
I'm just in such a rush today!"

The Imps confer, then they declare
That they can help the little bear.

The Imps lead Rupert down and down,
To their huge workshop underground.

They find a golden carriage there.
The Spring Imps polish it with care.

"It was an accident – I'm terribly sorry," Rupert begins. "There's a race tomorrow and I'm in a hurry to get home to find some wheels for my kart!" Rupert gestures towards the crate. The Imps begin to whisper. Rupert perches on his crate, and wonders glumly if they will drag him before the Imp King. "We accept your apology," they finally tell him. "And we can help you." The Imps open a secret trapdoor in the ground and leap inside, beckoning for Rupert to follow them.

Surprised, Rupert climbs down through the trapdoor and follows them along an earthy underground tunnel. After lots of twists and turns he emerges into a huge workshop. Imps are running to and fro, tending to a gleaming carriage that must surely belong to the Imp King himself! They seem to be replacing the wheels and look very busy. Then the Imp King comes to speak with Rupert. "I hear you have caused something of a commotion," he says sternly.

RUPERT IS GIVEN SOME WHEELS

And then they meet the Impish King,
And Rupert tells him everything.

"You need some wheels? Here's an idea!"
The Imp King says: "Take these wheels here!"

The King's old wheels will do just fine
If Bingo fixes them in time!

And Rupert is relieved to hear
His old pal Bingo say, "No fear!"

Rupert apologises again and explains about his go-kart, and the King forgives him. "I can help you," he tells Rupert. "I have just had new wheels put on my carriage, and have these old ones to spare." An Imp rushes forwards, carrying four wheels. "One wheel is buckled, but that should be easy enough to fix. These will do nicely for your go-kart," the King finishes. "Thank you, your Majesty!" Rupert cries. "I'm sure my friend will be able to fix the buckle!" Rupert does not notice the Imps smiling slyly.

The Imps see Rupert back up to the trapdoor. Rupert thanks them again and waves goodbye, dragging the wheels away in the crate and being very careful to avoid the grass and flowers. He heads straight for Bingo's house, where he finds his pal pottering around in his shed. Rupert hands the wheel over immediately and explains his predicament. "Can you fix it?" Rupert asks eagerly as Bingo studies it. "No fear," Bingo smiles. "I have just the thing!" He points to a machine in the corner of the shed.

RUPERT BUILDS HIS KART

Now Bingo drops a heavy plate
Which helps to set the bent wheel straight.

But as it works, they get a fright.
The room's lit up with sparks of light!

They fizzle and die out, and so
The pals both shrug, and off they go.

Kind Mr Bear's one step ahead,
He's fetched his tools out from the shed!

"This machine will straighten anything out," Bingo smiles. He places the wheel in between two large metal plates, then cranks a lever and presses the plates together. Strange brightly-coloured sparks and stars fly off the wheel as it is straightened. The friends jump back in fright! Whatever can be causing that? They think it is very odd, but after a moment the sparks stop, and they shrug. They are too excited to get on with building the go-kart to give it much thought.

A moment later, Bingo lifts the lever again and the plates come apart. The wheel looks as good as new and Rupert is delighted! "Thank you, Bingo! Now I can build my go-kart!" he says happily. The pair find a trolley and wheel the crate and wheels over to Rupert's garden. "Hello!" Mr Bear greets them cheerily. Mr Bear has heard about the go-kart project from Mrs Bear, and is waiting for them, tools at the ready. Rupert is very glad of his help.

RUPERT IS WHISKED AWAY

*No time to waste! They make a start
On building Rupert's racing kart.*

*And finally their work is done.
Now they can take it for a run.*

*The go-kart shoots into the air
And gives poor Rupert quite a scare!*

*The go-kart simply won't respond.
"Oh, help! I'm heading for that pond!"*

The three of them set to work building Rupert's go-kart. When it is finally finished, they stand back and admire their work. Rupert is very pleased and he jumps in, eager to test it out.

"What do you say we pay Edward a visit, to show him my go-kart?" Rupert smiles, gesturing for his friend to hop in. But before Bingo can lift a foot, the go-kart shudders and lurches forward, sparks shooting from the wheels.

As if it is alive, the go-kart launches into the air. "Help!" Rupert cries as he flails about in surprise. Mr Bear and Bingo can only watch in alarm as Rupert is taken higher and higher. The go-kart zooms over the garden hedge and away down the lane, and a moment later Rupert finds himself descending towards a pond in a nearby field. The go-kart skims across the pond surface, splashing Rupert and startling a sleepy duck.

Rupert and the Go-Kart Race

RUPERT IS TAKEN UNDERWATER

Beneath the water Rupert goes,
Where fish swim by and pond weed grows.

And he does not know if or when
He'll get back to dry land again!

The go-kart flies into the air,
And gives poor Rupert's friends a scare!

"It's magic! Help! Get me out, quick!
The Imps are playing quite a trick!"

A moment later the runaway go-kart dives under the water with an enormous splash! Rupert finds himself being pulled along through pond weed and fish, hanging on to the back of the go-kart for dear life! He wants to let go of the go-kart but he is too afraid. He squeezes his eyes shut, hoping that the go-kart will take him back above the surface in a moment. He has no idea what is happening or what the go-kart might do next!

To Rupert's relief, the go-kart shoots out of the pond and back into the air. It heads for Edward's garden, where Edward and Algy are admiring Edward's kart. "I must try to get back to the Imps!" Rupert gasps as he hurtles towards his friends. They see Rupert approaching, and jump out of the way in surprise as the kart swoops over their heads. "Help!" cries Rupert. "The Imps are playing a trick!" But before his pals can grab him, the go-kart soars upwards again.

RUPERT FLIES PAST A BALLOON

But Rupert's whisked away once more.
Into the sky the go-kart soars!

He flies right past an air balloon.
Is Rupert heading for the moon?

But no, he's taken to the tree
Where Imps are laughing merrily.

The go-kart will no longer fly,
And Rupert says a glad goodbye.

Rupert spots Podgy below him. "Help me!" Rupert shouts, waving frantically at his friend. But the go-kart is climbing higher and higher, and Rupert finds himself flying alongside a hot air balloon. The balloonist can't believe his eyes!

"Oh, my! Am I heading for the moon?" Rupert wonders. But the go-kart seems to be descending towards the common, and a moment later it lands bumpily next to the Imps' tree, where the Imps are falling about with laughter.

"Whatever is the matter with these wheels?" Rupert gasps. "They're magic!" one of the Imps replies. "They take the King anywhere he asks to go. But they've been misbehaving. The carriage crash-landed yesterday, so we had to remove them." Rupert sighs. "Well, I probably deserve it," he replies. The Imps remove the wheels and disappear underground. They emerge a moment later, promising that they have removed all the magic. Rupert thanks them and sets off home.

RUPERT AND PALS MEET BEFORE THE RACE

"Now, what I need's an early night
Before the race. But what's that light?"

And Rupert is surprised to see
Imps hanging bunting in the trees!

The pals meet up when morning comes,
And Rupert tells all to his chums.

"Look! I can see Jerome!" he cries.
"Yes! And the film crew!" Bill replies.

Rupert is exhausted after his adventures and needs an early night! He explains what happened to his parents, then Mr Bear helps him reattach the wheels before bed. As Rupert is drawing his curtains he spies some strange flashing lights in the sky. Curious, he sneaks out rund follows them to the common, where he is surprised to see the Imps decorating the trees with bunting. It must be for the race! Rupert smiles, and sneaks away before they see him.

The next morning, the chums gather before the race to hear about Rupert's runaway go-kart. Rupert tells them the whole thrilling tale, and they all have a good laugh together. Suddenly they hear the roar of an engine – it is Jerome, the friendly racing driver, and he has the television crew with him! "Mr Chimp told me about your race, and I've come to watch!" Jerome explains. The pals are delighted. The television crew are going to film the race – they will be on television!

"Now take this banger," says the bear,
"And pull it quickly through the air!"

The karts set off at racing speed
And Rupert's kart is in the lead!

But yet again, to his dismay,
The go-kart's whisking him away.

Now Rupert must use all his force
To steer the go-kart back on course.

Rupert shows Jerome his paper banger. "We need someone to start the race for us with this. Would you mind?" Jerome is very happy to help, and the pals line up at the start line. They are excited to see a small crowd has come to watch, no doubt intrigued by the sight of the television crew. Jerome positions himself at the side of the course. He drags the paper banger through the air and with a terrific bang they are off! Rupert immediately pulls into the lead.

But Podgy is catching up, and Rupert's go-kart is behaving oddly again – some of the magic has accidentally been left in the wheels! He struggles to control the go-kart, but it veers off the course into a copse. Rupert hurtles through the trees, struggling with the go-kart. After a few minutes he is able to steer it back onto the track. To his delight he sees he is neck and neck with Podgy! Rupert grits his teeth and does his best driving, hoping the wheels will behave for a few minutes.

Young Rupert's kart now ends the race
And fair and square, he's won first place!

As Rupert hears the crowd's loud cheers,
Into the sky he disappears!

And Mr Bear's surprised to see
Young Rupert flying on TV!

At bedtime, Rupert tells his Dad
Of the adventures that he's had.

The pals fly round the last few twists and turns of the track together. It is a very close race, but Rupert is first over the finish line and wins the race fair and square! Jerome and the television crew cheer loudly with the crowds. But the go-kart is not quite finished – it gives another great lurch and a shower of sparks fly off the wheels. With that, it takes off into the sky again. The television crew take off after the go-kart as it treats Rupert to a victory lap around Nutwood!

Mr Bear is amazed to see Rupert flying on television! And Rupert is enjoying himself. "Take me home!" he shouts to the wheels. A minute later the go-kart lands bumpily outside his house. Mr Bear rushes out, puts the go-kart safely away in the shed and leads an exhausted Rupert inside. Later that evening Mr Bear puts Rupert to bed and he tells his daddy his tale. "I'd very much like to be a racing driver when I grow up," he murmurs sleepily. "What a fun day it's been!"

One winter morning Rupert's told
To wrap up well against the cold.

Something strange has happened to the Nutwood weather. Although there are only a few days left before Christmas, it still seems very mild. "Never mind, Rupert," says Mrs Bear. "You should still wrap up well before you go out. If the weather changes, you could get caught in a snowstorm!" "There's not much danger of that," smiles Mr Bear. "The barometer says we'll have fine weather for the rest of the week …"

he Missing Snow

*"The weather's mild, but even so
This time of year, there could be snow!"*

*Soon Rupert spots his best pals, who
Are all wrapped up in thick coats too ...*

All Rupert's friends are wearing their winter coats too. "Phew!" gasps Algy. "It's jolly hot to be wrapped up like this!" "I do hope it snows soon!" says Willie Mouse. "I've written asking Santa for a pair of skis!" "I've asked for some ice skates," says Bill. "They won't be much use if the lake doesn't freeze!" "I asked for a sledge," adds Rupert. "Unless it snows, I won't be able to use that either ..."

*The chums explain the reasons they
Hope that it snows by Christmas Day.*

John Harold.

"The weather forecast's very strange,"
Says Mr Bear. "It says 'No change'!"

That evening Rupert wakes to hear
A tapping sound from somewhere near . . .

It's Santa's Little Cowboy who
Says, "Rupert! I've been sent for you ..."

As soon as Rupert's ready he
Runs to the plane. "Quick, follow me!"

When Rupert goes home for tea that afternoon, he tells his parents how disappointed his pals will be if the weather doesn't get colder. "It's certainly very odd!" says Mr Bear. "The forecast still says 'fine'. If anything, it seems to be getting even milder ..." In the evenings, when Rupert goes to bed, he lies awake and thinks how dull Christmas will be if it doesn't snow at all. He is just drifting off to sleep when he suddenly hears someone tapping at the window ...

Opening the window and peering out, Rupert is surprised to see his friend, the Little Cowboy. "Sorry to wake you," he whispers. "Santa's sent me to ask if you can join us at once ..." "Of course!" says Rupert. "But what's the matter?" "No time to explain!" says the Cowboy. "He'll tell you himself as soon as we arrive ..." Slipping quietly out of the house, Rupert follows the Cowboy to the edge of the common. "This way!" he calls and points to his plane.

RUPERT VISITS SANTA'S CASTLE

The pair take off and quickly fly
To Santa's castle in the sky.

The Little Cowboy leads the way
To Santa Claus without delay.

It's warm in Santa's office too –
"This winter sun will never do!"

"I need someone like you to go
And ask the Weather Clerk for snow."

Rupert climbs aboard the little plane and is soon flying north through the night sky. "That's where we're heading for!" calls the Cowboy, and points to a cloud that seems to glow on the horizon. As the plane gets nearer, Rupert sees the towers of a castle, bathed in dazzling light. The Cowboy lands in the castle courtyard and hurries to the main gate. "Special visitor for Santa!" he tells the sentries. "Come on, Rupert. I'll take you to see him straightaway ..."

The Little Cowboy leads the way to Santa's office and knocks at the door. "Come in!" calls a loud voice. "Ah, Rupert! Just the person I wanted to see ..." Mopping his brow with a handkerchief, Santa explains that he's worried about the mild weather. "Unless it snows soon, lots of children will be disappointed!" he declares. "I must get the Clerk of the Weather to find out what's wrong, but I'm too busy to go and see him. Perhaps you can go instead?"

RUPERT MEETS THE WEATHER CLERK

Rupert agrees to help and then
Takes off into the sky again.

"The weather station!" Rupert cries.
"And there's someone I recognise ..."

The Clerk and his Assistant hear
How there has been no snow this year.

The Clerk takes down a weighty book –
"I'm sure I sent some snow. Yes, look!"

Rupert agrees to do as Santa asks, and follows the Little Cowboy back to his plane. They take off and are soon flying through a dark, star-spangled sky. Just as Rupert is wondering how they will ever find their way, he sees a pale silver light in the distance. "Weather Station ahead!" calls the Cowboy. The plane gets nearer and Rupert can see someone waving. "It's the Weather Clerk's Assistant!" he cries. "He must have seen your plane and come to meet us ..."

As soon as Rupert explains what's wrong, the Assistant summons his master. "No snow?" says the Clerk. "But I'm sure we sent some!" He hurries inside and pulls down a huge ledger. "There! Snow for Nutwood. Sent from the North Pole last week!" "The North Pole?" asks Rupert. "Yes," the Assistant explains. "Snow clouds are stored there. It acts as a magnet and keeps them safe until they're needed." "Don't worry!" says the Clerk. "I'll send more snow immediately ..."

RUPERT IS DISAPPOINTED

As Rupert flies back home he's sure
That it will snow, the Clerk's sent more.

On Christmas Eve he waits all day
But there's no sign snow's on the way ...

Next morning, Rupert wakes to see
There's still *no snow. Where can it be?*

Rupert unwraps his sledge to find
A note that Santa's left behind.

"Let's hope the snow *arrives* this time!" says the Little Cowboy as they fly back from the Weather Station. It has started to grow light by the time they reach Nutwood and Rupert has to hurry to be sure of getting home before anyone is awake. All day long he keeps looking out of the window, but as evening falls and he helps to finish decorating the Christmas tree, there is *still* no sign of snow. "How odd," he thinks. "The Clerk promised to send some straightaway!"

When Rupert wakes on Christmas Day, he leaps out of bed and hurries to draw the curtains. "Oh, no!" he cries, as he peers out of the window. "It hasn't snowed at all ..." At the foot of his bed is a large, bulky parcel, which turns out to be a new sledge. Tucked inside the wrapping paper, Rupert finds a note from Santa: "Missing snow more serious than first suspected. Need your help urgently. Little Cowboy will meet you by edge of common. Wear warm clothes ..."

RUPERT JOINS AN EXPEDITION

He hurries to the common where
The Clerk's Assistant's waiting there ...

"We have to find the missing snow,"
He says to Rupert as they go.

"The North Pole's where the snow should be,
We store it there in clouds, you see!"

"That's odd! My computer says that we're
At the North Pole, but nothing's here!"

The moment breakfast is over, Rupert puts on his coat and runs to the common. Waiting there is the Little Cowboy and the Weather Clerk's Assistant. "Something's wrong with the weather controls!" the Assistant says. "Hop aboard and I'll tell you all about it ..." As the plane leaves Nutwood, he explains how the extra snow clouds he sent to the North Pole were mysteriously blown off course. "That's where we're going now," he adds. "To find out what happened ..."

On and on the little plane flies, further and further north. The air grows cold and frosty. "Look!" cries Rupert as he spots icebergs floating in the water below. "Right on course!" declares the Assistant and begins to direct the Cowboy towards the Pole. After a while, he stops giving directions and peers anxiously at his compass. "I don't understand!" he tells Rupert. "According to my map, we should have reached the Pole, but all I can see is ice and snow!"

RUPERT MEETS HIS UNCLE POLAR

"My Uncle Polar!" Rupert cries.
"He's bound to know where the Pole lies!"

"Look! There's his house. Let's go and see.
I'm sure that he'll remember me ..."

His two companions come as well
As Rupert goes to ring the bell.

A polar bear appears. "Bless me!"
"Is that my nephew that I see?"

"Let's go back and try again," suggests the Little Cowboy. "No," says the Assistant. "There's nothing there. I'm sure we didn't miss it ..." Just as it seems they will have to give up their search, Rupert suddenly remembers his Uncle Polar. "Of course!" he cries. "My uncle lives somewhere near here. Let's ask him to help us." The others agree and fly on until a solitary igloo comes into sight. "That's his house," calls Rupert. "Land outside and I'll introduce you both."

The plane taxis to a halt on the frozen snow and Rupert hurries towards the igloo. He rings the bell and waits for a reply. At first nothing happens, then a huge white bear peers out from the narrow doorway. "Uncle Polar!" cries Rupert. "Bless me!" laughs his uncle. "What a pleasant surprise! How nice to see you, Rupert, but what brings you to this part of the world? Come inside and tell me all about it. Bring your friends too," he adds. "There's plenty of room ..."

RUPERT STAYS IN AN IGLOO

Although the igloo looks quite small,
Inside it isn't cramped at all ...

"You'll have to stay this evening, so
I'll ring your folks and let them know."

Next morning the Assistant brings
His compass as they pack their things.

"No need!" smiles Polar. "For I know
Exactly where we've got to go!"

"Come and sit down," says Uncle Polar. "You must be tired after such a long journey!" He listens carefully as Rupert describes the search for the North Pole. "It's not always easy to find," he says. "Why don't you stay overnight and let me take you in the morning?" "I've got to get back to Santa," says the Cowboy. "You two stay and I'll come to fetch you tomorrow ..." Rupert agrees and asks his Uncle Polar to telephone Nutwood and let his parents know he is safe and sound.

The next day, Uncle Polar is up bright and early, making preparations for the expedition. "We've got a long walk ahead of us," he tells Rupert. "It's a good idea to take a picnic lunch." "I'll bring my compass too!" declares the Assistant. "Would you like to borrow my map?" "No need for that," smiles Uncle Polar. "I already know the way to the Pole ..." When everyone is wrapped up well, he opens the door of the igloo and leads the way out across the snow ...

RUPERT SEES THE POLE IS MISSING

Across the snow, he starts to stride
Due North, with Rupert at his side.

But as the trio march along
The Assistant's sure something's wrong ...

"Good gracious!" Uncle Polar cries,
Unable to believe his eyes ...

"The mound that we're all standing on
Is the right place – but the Pole's gone!"

As they leave the igloo behind them and march through the crisp, white snow, Rupert asks his uncle how he manages to find the way. "It's easy when you know what to look for," he laughs. "All you have to do is follow your nose!" "Pardon me for asking," says the Assistant, "but are you sure we're still going in the right direction? My compass is pointing more to the West ..."

"Nonsense!" growls Uncle Polar. "There must be something wrong with it! We're almost there ..."

As the three companions continue on their way, it is Uncle Polar's turn to look puzzled. He stops, peers into the distance, walks a few paces forward, then comes to a complete halt. "It's gone!" he cries. "Sorry?" asks Rupert. "The North Pole!" gasps Uncle Polar. "It's been here since I was a cub. Now it's ... disappeared!" Sure enough, when they reach the spot where the Pole should stand, there is nothing to be seen but a small hole in the ice!

RUPERT'S UNCLE HAS AN IDEA

*"Look!" Rupert cries. "Someone's been here.
Their footprints still look very clear."*

*"Thieves!" Polar growls. "I'm sure that they
Removed the Pole and sailed away!"*

*"We'll find them!" the Assistant cries.
"My compass still shows where it lies …"*

*"Good! Polar cries. "Now, follow me!
We'll chase their boat across the sea …"*

What can have happened to the North Pole? As his uncle stares at the hole in the ice, Rupert spots a trail of footprints. "Look!" he cries. "Someone's been here before us!" "You don't think they took the Pole?" gasps the Assistant. "We'll soon find out!" growls Uncle Polar and starts to follow the tracks across the snow. To Rupert's surprise, they come to a sudden halt, where the ice meets the open sea. "Hrrumph!" cries Uncle Polar. "They must have left here in a boat!"

"If only *we* had a boat!" groans the Assistant. "Then we'd be able to follow them! My compass is still pointing towards the Pole, you see. All we have to do to find out what's been taken is to keep going in the same direction …" "You're right!" cries Uncle Polar. "But there's no need for a boat, just follow me!" With that, he leaps across to a large ice floe that's floating nearby. "Come on!" he calls to Rupert. "There's plenty of room here for us all!"

RUPERT SAILS ON AN ICE FLOE

*The pair jump on, but neither know
How Polar plans to use the floe ...*

*Then, from his pocket, Polar brings
A little bell he kneels and rings ...*

*Up pops a walrus, Wallace, who
Asks Polar what he wants to do.*

*He pushes them along as they
Use the compass to find the way.*

With the Assistant's compass to point the way, Uncle Polar seems sure that they will find the missing Pole. "Well done!" he cries as Rupert jumps across to join him. "This ice floe will make a splendid boat!" "Of course!" gasps the Assistant. "But how will you make it go in the right direction?" "Don't worry about that," laughs Polar and pulls a little silver bell from his pocket. "Quiet now," he whispers and starts to ring it, just above the water's surface.

For a long time nothing happens. Then there is a sudden splash and up pops a huge walrus! "This is an old friend of mine, called Wallace," explains Uncle Polar and tells the walrus all about the missing Pole and how they hope to find it again. "Happy to help you!" cries Wallace and starts to push against the ice floe with all his might. Soon the friends are gliding through the water, with the Assistant giving directions while Rupert keeps watch for any strange ships.

RUPERT SPOTS A SHIP

Ahead of them they spot a boat
Above which snow clouds seem to float ...

No wonder that the ship's so slow,
Its decks are thick with ice and snow!

As Uncle Polar climbs aboard
The crew run off. "A bear that roared!"

Then Rupert spots a look out, who
Has been forgotten by the crew ...

Peering into the distance, Rupert spots some menacing dark clouds. The compass is pointing straight towards what looks like a giant snowstorm! "I can see a ship on the horizon!" he calls suddenly. "You're right!" gasps Uncle Polar. "Quick, Wallace! We mustn't lose sight of it!" As they draw nearer to the strange ship, Rupert can see that its decks are covered in a thick layer of snow. "How odd!" he murmurs. "It looks as if the blizzard has been following her for days ..."

The ship is so heavily laden with snow that it can hardly move through the water. "Push us alongside, Wallace," calls Uncle Polar and gets ready to clamber aboard. As soon as they see him the sailors give a cry of alarm and run for their cabins as fast as they can. "Come back!" calls Uncle Polar, but by the time the Assistant and Rupert have joined him on deck there is no-one to be seen. No-one, that is, except a young look-out, who peers nervously down from the rigging.

RUPERT FINDS THE NORTH POLE

*"Don't be afraid!" says Rupert. "We
Must see your captain urgently ..."*

*The Captain peers around the door
But dares not come out any more.*

*"I only want to let you know –
The North Pole's what attracts this snow!"*

*The Captain blinks. "I'd no idea!
In that case you can have it. Here!"*

"I don't know why everyone ran away!" shrugs Uncle Polar. "Never mind," says Rupert. "Let's talk to the look-out." Telling the boy not to be frightened, Rupert asks him how long the ship has been caught in the blizzard. "Ever since the captain came back from the North Pole," replies the boy. Rupert smiles and asks him to take them to the Captain's cabin. "Visitors, sir!" calls the boy. The door opens a crack and the Captain peers out anxiously ...

"I hear you've been to the North Pole," says Uncle Polar sternly. "Y ... yes," replies the Captain. "I'm an explorer." "And you've taken the Pole as a souvenir!" cries Rupert. "How did you know?" gasps the Captain. "Because it's a snow magnet," says Rupert. "That's why there's a blizzard following your ship ..." The Captain blinks in astonishment. "I had no idea! In that case, you're welcome to it! The sooner it's back in its rightful place, the better!"

RUPERT RETURNS THE POLE

"Goodbye!" the look out calls as he
Sees Rupert's ice floe put to sea.

The walrus pushes them once more
Across the water, to the shore.

"Thanks, Wallace!" Polar says, then he
Strides back to where the Pole should be.

He hands the Pole to Rupert when
It's time to put it back again ...

"We're ready to go now, Wallace!" calls Uncle Polar. Holding the Pole carefully, he clambers back over the ship's rail and is soon helping Rupert and the Assistant back on to the ice floe. "Goodbye!" calls the look-out as they begin to glide away from the ship. "And thank you for saving us from the blizzard ..." "We'll soon put things right now!" smiles Uncle Polar as the ice floe nears the shore. "Explorers indeed! Fancy trying to take the Pole home!"

As soon as the ice floe is near enough, Uncle Polar leaps off and helps the others to scramble ashore. "Well done, Wallace!" he tells his friend. "Without your help, we'd never have caught that ship!" Following the footprints back across the snow, he leads the way to the stone circle and hands the Pole to Rupert. "It's only right that you should put it back," he tells him. "If it hadn't been for you, no-one would have realised what was wrong." "Bravo!" cries the Assistant.

RUPERT FLIES BACK

Then Polar telephones to tell
Santa that things have turned out well ...

The Little Cowboy's plane appears.
"I hear you've found the Pole!" he cheers.

"Goodbye!" waves Rupert's uncle. Then
The little plane flies off again.

"That must be the explorer's ship.
Now they've escaped the snowstorm's grip ..."

As soon as the North Pole is safely back in place, Uncle Polar sets off across the snow towards his cosy igloo. While Rupert and the Assistant have a warm drink, he telephones Santa Claus to let him know that the mystery of the missing snow has been solved. "Splendid news!" says Santa. "I'll send the Little Cowboy to collect Rupert and his friend." Before long, Rupert hears the sound of a plane approaching and hurries out to see the Little Cowboy coming in to land.

"Goodbye, Rupert!" calls Uncle Polar as the plane takes off. "Glad I was able to help. Come and see me again soon!" Rupert promises that he will and waves to his uncle as the Little Cowboy flies off over the frozen snow and ice. "Look!" cries Rupert as they head out to sea. "There's the explorer's ship!" No longer icebound, the ship has at last escaped from the blizzard and is sailing steadily south. "I wonder if the look-out can see us?" thinks Rupert and waves at the ship.

RUPERT TRIES HIS NEW SLEDGE

The Weather Clerk tells Rupert how
The snow's heading for Nutwood now.

The Cowboy cries, "Let's go and see!"
And off they fly immediately ...

As Nutwood reappears below
The sky is full of falling snow!

The Cowboy stays behind and tries
Out Rupert's sledge. "Yippee!" he cries.

Flying up above the clouds, the Little Cowboy carries on until he spots the distant towers of the Weather Station. The Clerk of the Weather is delighted to hear that the North Pole is back in place and tells Rupert that the clouds he sent should be well on their way to Nutwood. After saying goodbye to the Assistant, Rupert and the Cowboy climb into the plane and take off once more. "It won't be long before you're home!" calls the Cowboy as they start to gather speed.

"Look!" cries Rupert excitedly as Nutwood comes into view. "It's started snowing at last!" Down below he spots some of his pals, who are busy making a snowman. As soon as the plane lands he runs home to fetch his new sledge. "Come on!" he calls to the Little Cowboy. "Let's both go and try it out ..." "Yippee!" cries the Cowboy as the pair whizz downhill. "If your Uncle Polar was here, I think he'd feel right at home!"

The End.

Rupert Annual Reader Survey 2014

We'd love to know what you think about your Rupert Annual.

Fill in this form and post it to the address at the end
by 28th February 2014, or you can fill in the survey online at:
www.egmont.co.uk/rupertsurvey2014

Children should ask an adult to help them with this.

One lucky reader will win £150 of book tokens.
Five runners up will win a £25 book token each.

1. Who bought this annual?

☐ Me

☐ Parent/guardian

☐ Grandparent

☐ Other (please specify)

....

2. Why did they buy it?

☐ Christmas present

☐ Birthday present

☐ I'm a collector

☐ Other (please specify)

....

3. What are your favourite parts of the Rupert Annual?

Stories	☐ Really like	☐ Like	☐ Don't like
Activities	☐ Really like	☐ Like	☐ Don't like

4. Do you think the stories are too long, too short or about right?

☐ Too long   ☐ Too short   ☐ About right

5. Do you think the activities are too hard, too easy or about right?

☐ Too hard   ☐ Too easy   ☐ About right

6. Apart from Rupert, who are your favourite characters?

1. ....

2. ....

3. ....

7. Which other annuals do you like?

1. ....

2. ....

3. ....

8. What is your favourite …

1. … app or website? ....

2. … console game? ....

3. … magazine? ....

4. … book? ....

9. What are your favourite TV programmes?

1. ....

2. ....

3. ....

10. Would you like to get the Rupert Annual again next year?

☐ Yes   ☐ No

Why? ....

....

Name: .... Age:................... Boy ☐ Girl ☐

Signature: ....

Email address: ....

Daytime telephone number: ....

☐ Please send me the Egmont Monthly Catch-Up Newsletter.

Please cut out and post to:

Rupert Annual Reader Survey, Egmont UK Limited, The Yellow Building, 1 Nicholas Road, London, W11 4AN   *Good luck!*